Children's Authors

Tomie dePaola

Mae Woods
ABDO Publishing Company

visit us at
www.abdopub.com

Published by ABDO Publishing Company, 4940 Viking Drive, Suite 622, Edina, Minnesota 55435. Copyright © 2000 Abdo Consulting Group, Inc., Pentagon Tower, P.O. Box 36036, Minneapolis, Minnesota 55435 USA. International copyrights reserved in all countries. No part of this book may be reproduced in any form without written permission from the publisher.

Published 2000
Printed in the United States of America
Second Printing 2002

Photos: AP/Wideworld, Corbis
Editors: Bob Italia, Tamara L. Britton, Kate A. Furlong
Art Direction: Pat Laurel

Library of Congress Cataloging-in-Publication Data

Woods, Mae.
   Tomie dePaola / Mae Woods.
     p. cm. -- (Children's authors)
   Includes Bibliographical references (p.) and index.
   Summary: Presents the life of the author-illustrator who has won numerous awards and prizes, including the Caldecott Medal, for his children's books.
   ISBN 1-57765-114-6
   1. dePaola, Tomie--Juvenile literature. 2. Authors, American--20th century--Biography--Juvenile literature. 3. Illustrators--United States-- Biography--Juvenile literature. 4. Children's stories--Authorship--Juvenile literature. [1. dePaola, Tomie. 2. Authors, American. 3. Illustrators.] I. Title

PS3554.E1147 Z95 2000
813'.54--dc21
[B]   99-088857

Second printing 2002

Contents

Tomie's Family

*T*homas Anthony dePaola was born in Meriden, Connecticut, on September 15, 1934. His parents were Joseph and Florence dePaola. His mother was called Flossie. Flossie's parents, Thomas and Alice Downey, were from Ireland. Joseph's parents, Antonio and Concetta dePaola, were from Italy.

Tomie had an older brother, Joseph Jr., who was called Buddy. He also had two younger sisters, Maureen and Judie. The dePaola home was always filled with activity.

On Sundays, Tomie's family visited his Irish grandparents. Tom Downey was an entertaining storyteller. The family gathered around the kitchen table and listened to tales of relatives in "the old country" and gossip from the grocery store he ran in town.

Tomie's mother read stories to him at night. He liked to draw pictures to go with the stories. When Tomie was four years old, he knew he wanted to be a storybook artist.

Meriden, Connecticut, shortly before Tomie was born

Early Years

*T*omie's father had a movie camera. He used it to make home movies. Young Tomie loved to perform for the camera. He turned his sandbox upside down and used it as a stage.

In 1940, Tomie began taking dancing lessons. Tomie often appeared on stage at school or sang in church. He loved to tap dance, especially when he could dress in fancy costumes. In 1944, his dance group was invited to perform in New York City.

Tomie's parents encouraged his interest in art and performing. They allowed him to create a work space in the attic. There, he made puppets and **designed** a stage for puppet shows.

During his school years, Tomie became a **confident** performer and artist. He loved high school, except for gym class! It was a very special time in his life. In 1952, Tomie graduated from high school.

New York City is an exciting place to visit.

College Days

*T*omie's twin cousins Franny and Fuffy McLaughlin were photographers. They went to Pratt Art Institute in New York. Tomie wanted to study there, too. He applied for a **scholarship** and was accepted.

In September of 1952, Tomie's parents helped him move into a **dormitory** at Pratt. Tomie took classes from 9 A.M. to 5 P.M. It was just like going to a job. He also had lots of homework every night. His busy schedule taught Tomie good work habits.

Two of the first lessons Tomie learned were to observe everything and practice drawing as much as he could. So, he carried a **sketchbook** with him wherever he went.

Tomie watched people and practiced drawing them. He learned how to look at things with an artist's "inner eye." The "inner eye" uses feelings and imagination as well as sight.

When he could, Tomie went to the Museum of Modern Art on Saturdays to watch old silent movies and study the paintings on exhibit. This exposed him to new styles of painting. One of his favorite artists was French painter Georges Rouault.

In 1955, Tomie spent the summer in Maine studying at the Skowhegan School of Painting and Sculpture. Ben Shahn, a famous painter, was a teacher there. Shahn encouraged Tomie and inspired him to work hard.

Ben Shahn

Getting Started

*I*n 1956, Tomie graduated from college. As a graduation gift, his parents gave him a trip to Europe. He traveled to Spain, Portugal, Italy, Switzerland, and France. It was exciting for Tomie to see works of art that he had only seen in books.

Getting started on a career was difficult. There were so many things Tomie wanted to do. He loved painting and performing. He also thought about becoming a **monk**. In October of 1956, he went to live in a **monastery**. But Tomie decided he wanted to do other things. He left the monastery after six months.

For several years, Tomie did many different things. He **designed** Christmas cards. He worked in summer theater. He painted, and taught art classes. He liked these jobs, but he still wanted to **pursue** his early dream of illustrating children's books. In 1963, Tomie illustrated his first book, *Sound*, by Lisa Miller. Tomie discovered this was what he liked to do best of all.

Tomie lived in a monastery, such as this one.

An Artist and Writer

*T*he first books Tomie illustrated were written by other authors. But the **publisher** liked his work and asked him if he had any story ideas of his own. Of course, he did.

The first book Tomie wrote was *The Wonderful Dragon of Timlin*. Since then, he has written and illustrated almost 200 books.

Some of Tomie's books are funny. *Bill and Pete* tells the adventures of a crocodile and the bird that is his toothbrush. *Pancakes for Breakfast* is the tale of a woman trying to make her favorite meal. *Too Many Hopkins* shows how much trouble a family of 15 young rabbits can cause when they learn to plant a garden.

Tomie has written **nonfiction** books, too. The first was *Charlie Needs a Cloak*. Then he wrote *The Quicksand Book,* which shows how quicksand is formed. *The Cloud Book* teaches about clouds. And *The Popcorn Book* tells how to make popcorn. Tomie's nonfiction books use humor and lovable characters to make learning fun.

Tomie's favorite food is popcorn.

Memories

Some of Tomie's books are about his own childhood. *Nana Upstairs and Nana Downstairs* is about his visits to his grandmother Alice and her mother, Tomie's great grandmother. *Oliver Button Is a Sissy* is about a boy who would rather draw and dance than play sports. *Tom* and *Now One Foot, Now the Other* are about Tomie's Irish grandfather. *Watch Out for the Chicken Feet in Your Soup, The Art Lesson,* and *The Baby Sister* are also based on things that happened to him.

Other books include details from Tomie's life. One of his most popular books is the folk tale *Strega Nona.* Strega Nona comes from Calabria in Italy, just like Tomie's father's family. Readers loved the story of the overflowing pasta pot. In 1976, *Strega Nona* was a **Caldecott** Honor Book.

Readers wanted to read more about Big Anthony and the clever old "grandmother witch." So Tomie wrote more stories about them: *Strega Nona's Magic Lessons; Big Anthony and the Magic Ring; Merry Christmas, Strega Nona; Strega Nona Meets Her Match; Strega Nona, Her Story;* and *Big Anthony.*

Over 5 million copies of Tomie's books have been sold.

Doodling and Daydreaming

*T*omie thinks there should be a special class in school for "wasting time, **doodling,** and daydreaming." He gets his best ideas while he daydreams or **sketches**. He believes that everyone needs a quiet time to do nothing except imagine things. As a child, he listened to a radio show called *Let's Pretend*. Tomie thinks this helped him to **develop** his imagination.

Tomie gets ideas for stories from many different places. Not all of them are based on memories of his childhood. He reads a lot of books. He especially enjoys **folk tales**. These give him ideas for new stories or new ways to tell old stories.

Since art school, Tomie has thought it was important to observe people and animals. He has four Welsh terriers. Watching his dogs play might even give Tomie an idea for a story or a picture.

Tomie with his dogs

Tomie at Home

*T*omie lives in a farmhouse in New London, New Hampshire. He turned his 200-year-old barn into a three-story studio. He likes to have lots of space to work and to display his collection of early American **folk art**. His house has three kitchens because Tomie loves to cook. He has six ovens, a grill room, four refrigerators, and three dishwashers!

Christmas is Tomie's favorite holiday. He studies Christmas **traditions** from the past and from other countries. He combines different traditions to celebrate the holiday.

Tomie likes to bake at Christmas. He also loves to decorate the tree. He makes angels and pink paper roses. He adds hundreds of lights and special decorations that he has collected from all over the world. He decorates the house with **poinsettias** and evergreen branches and burns candles in his windows at night.

Opposite page: Tomie takes a break from writing to relax outside.

New Projects

*T*omie's first chapter book is titled *26 Fairmount Avenue*. This is the address of his family's first house. He remembers the excitement of watching the house being built. Tomie would borrow the carpenter's blue chalk and draw pictures of his family on the inside walls. Tomie lived in that house from kindergarten to adulthood. It is full of memories. Readers loved *26 Fairmount Avenue*. It was a 2000 **Newbery** Honor Book.

Tomie stays in touch with his readers. He visits classrooms. Tomie still loves to perform. Sometimes he reads his favorite stories in a theater accompanied by an **orchestra**. He also paints and exhibits his art work. Tomie has plans for many more books.

Tomie's second book about 26 Fairmount Avenue is **Here We All Are.**

Glossary

Caldecott Medal - an award given by the American Library Association to the author of the year's best picture book. Books that are runners-up are called Caldecott Honor Books.

confident - certain of being successful.

design - to plan and arrange something with artistic skill.

develop - to grow or expand.

doodling - scribbling or sketching without any purpose.

dormitory - a building with small rooms for students to live in.

folk art - the traditional art of literate societies by artists without traditional academic training.

folk tales - stories that are part of the beliefs, traditions, and customs of a people. Folk tales are handed down through generations.

monastery - a place where a group of monks live and work together.

monk - a religious man who lives in a monastery.

Newbery Award - an award given by the American Library Association to the author of the year's best children's book. Books that are runners-up are called Newbery Honor Books.

nonfiction - books based on true facts.

orchestra - a large group of musicians playing together.

poinsettia - a plant that has large red leaves.

publisher - someone who produces printed materials for sale to the public.

pursue - the act of following.

scholarship - a gift of money to help a student pay for instruction.

sketch - a quick drawing. Sketches are usually drawn on pads of paper called sketchbooks.

traditions - customs that are handed down to each new generation.

Internet Sites

Tomie dePaola

www.tomie.com

This is Tomie dePaola's official Web site. This informative site includes a biography and bibliography. Learn more about Tomie by reading the answers to frequently asked questions. Tomie's travel schedule is available; find out if he will visit your town!

Write to Tomie at:
Tomie dePaola
Penguin Putnam Books for Young Readers
345 Hudson Street
NY, NY 10014

Index